Street Furniture

Kenneth Hudson

Photographs by Ann Nicholls

THE BODLEY HEAD

LONDON SYDNEY
TORONTO

ACKNOWLEDGMENTS

Thanks are due to the following for supplying photographs: William Morris, page 45 (top); The Manx Museum and the National Trust, page 42; Bord Failte, page 43.

British Library Cataloguing
in Publication Data
Hudson, Kenneth
Street furniture
1. Streets–Great Britain–Accessories
–Juvenile literature
I. Title
620'.417'32   TE57
ISBN 0–370–30168–4

Printed and bound in Great Britain for
The Bodley Head Ltd
9 Bow Street, London WC2E 7AL
by Fakenham Press Ltd, Fakenham
set in Monophoto Ehrhardt
First published 1979

Contents

What we mean by 'street furniture'

When we talk of furniture, we usually mean things like chairs and tables and beds and cupboards. A street's furniture is different. It includes lamp-posts, litter bins, bus shelters, shop signs, signposts, manhole covers, pillar boxes, telephone booths, public lavatories, fountains and, of course, seats. These are the working parts of a street, the bits and pieces that help people to get around and make life more comfortable, convenient and safe.

Some of the street furniture we can still see doing a useful job today is very old. Up and down Britain there are plenty of pillar boxes, signposts, milestones, seats and public clocks that are more than a hundred years old. Many of the real veterans, like drinking troughs for horses and water-pumps, aren't needed any more, but they're reminders of how people used to live in the past, before the days of cars and electricity and telephones. To anyone who walks about with his or her eyes open, the streets are full of history.

Much of the really old street furniture has survived by accident, because it's off the beaten track, in side roads or alleys or quiet squares, or because it would be too difficult or cost too much to remove it or replace it with something more modern. Some museums have gone to a lot of trouble to preserve this kind of material. One of the best collections is at the Castle Museum in York, which has a series of carefully reconstructed Victorian streets in the museum, with fully stocked shops, workshops and pubs.

Using your eyes

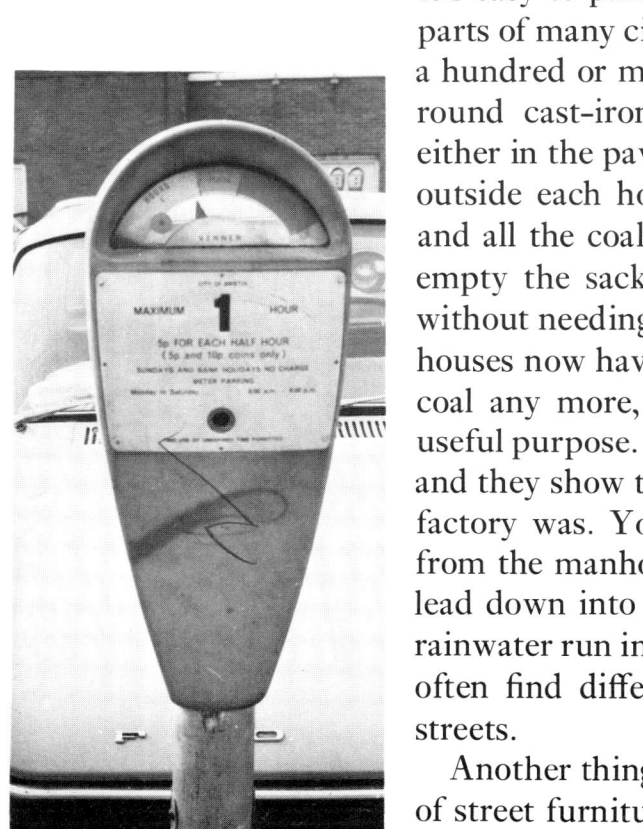

Much of the old street furniture has gone, but there is still plenty to see, if you know what you're looking for. Some of the most interesting items are very simple and it's easy to pass by without noticing them. In the older parts of many cities, where there are biggish houses built a hundred or more years ago, you can often see a row of round cast-iron plates, about eighteen inches across, either in the pavement or along the edge of the road, one outside each house. These were put above the cellars, and all the coalman had to do was lift up the plate and empty the sacks of coal straight down into the cellar, without needing to go into the house at all. Most of these houses now have gas or oil central heating and don't use coal any more, so these iron covers no longer serve a useful purpose. But a lot of them are beautifully designed and they show the maker's name and the place where his factory was. You can get the same sort of information from the manhole covers over the inspection shafts that lead down into the sewers, and from the grilles that let rainwater run into the drains. If you look carefully, you'll often find different manufacturers' names in different streets.

Another thing to watch out for is the number of pieces of street furniture that were presented to the city or the village by private people. These often carry the name of

the person involved. Fountains, seats, water-pumps, public clocks and horse-troughs were particular favourites for this kind of gift, but you'll notice local benefactors' names on other things as well, like public shelters in parks and on seafronts.

Nearly all street furniture is there because at one time or another there was a need for it, although sometimes you can see things which are just ornaments or advertisements. No two streets or towns have the same collection of street furniture. Life has developed in a different way in different parts of the country and people's needs are different. What's right for Penzance isn't necessarily right for Aberdeen or Swansea. In Birmingham or Edinburgh, it's much easier for a motorist to get lost than it is in Barnstaple or Crewe, so the signposting has to be that much better. A seaside town needs more litter bins and more public lavatories, at least in the summer, than the centre of Manchester or Wolverhampton does. A busy city needs pedestrian crossings more than a village does. So, when we're looking at the street furniture in any town, no matter what its size, it's useful and interesting to ask, 'What sort of place is this? What goes on here – or what used to go on here? Why does it have the kind of street furniture that it does?'

Names and signs

Street names

Without street signs, only the natives would be able to find their way about a town. The simplest type of sign is painted on the wall, but this has to be replaced or touched up fairly often, and for two hundred years the usual method has been to put the name up in cast iron or tiles. At one time these signs were made locally, so that each district had its own design, but nowadays they follow standard patterns and are less interesting and less beautiful. Sometimes the names were carved into the stone of the buildings themselves.

You can find out a great deal about a town or village from its street names. Many of them commemorate famous local inhabitants, others provide clues to occupations and industries which used to be carried on there at one time and to important buildings which stood there once, but have since been pulled down. So we have names like Castle Street, Haymarket, Mill Lane, Tan Yard, Ship Street, Brick Lane, Theatre Street, Station Street, and so on. You can almost write the history of a town from its street names.

House and shop numbers

Painting has been the favourite way of doing this. The numbers are painted on the gateposts or walls, on the nameboard above the shop or often, on eighteenth- and nineteenth-century houses, on the fanlights above the front doors.

A more usual way of doing the job from about 1850 onwards, was to have the numbers painted on enamel plates, which could be screwed to the door, or to have the numbers cut out or cast in metal and then screwed on.

Inn signs

These are one of the oldest kinds of street furniture. They have been in common use in Britain for more than five hundred years. Until recently, they were painted by artists who specialised in the work and who travelled round the country to practise their craft on the spot. Nowadays, when most public houses belong to big brewing groups, the usual system is to take the signs back to a central workshop for repair and repainting, which takes away a lot of the originality and local style that used to be found in the old days. But, even now, inn signs, like trade signs and advertisements, do a great deal to liven up the street scene and they are an interesting link with the past. We have had Elephants and Castles, Red Lions, Marquis of Granbys, Bulls and Bushes and King's Arms for generations. Many inn signs recall local trades, past and present – the Steelworkers' Arms, the Miners' Arms – and others local worthies – the Daniel Gooch at Swindon, for instance, commemorates the Great Western Railway locomotive designer. In many instances, an inn sign is all there is to remind us of a feature of the district that no longer exists. There are a number of Canal Inns, for example, in places where the canal has long since been filled in, and Railway Hotels and Station Hotels where the line was closed years ago.

Milestones

The ancestors of milestones in Britain were what are known as pudding stones, so called because they were made of a kind of speckled stone looking rather like a plum pudding. They were about three feet high and narrower at the top than the bottom. The earliest of them, dating from about 5000 BC, were probably used to mark tribal meeting places, as well as to measure distances. Some of these stones can still be seen in the South of England. Sometimes they have been built into the walls of cottages and churches.

The Romans put up a great many milestones along the main roads of their empire. Between sixty and seventy of them survive in Britain, mostly in museums, although a few are on their original site.

Many later milestones are difficult to date. After the General Turnpike Act of 1773 it was compulsory to put the mileage on milestones or signposts, but before that many of them gave only the direction, such as 'The road to Hereford'. Some eighteenth-century milestones were known as 'shy' milestones, because they were shy of giving exact information. Only local people would know along the Oxford to London road, for instance, that 'The City' meant London, 'The University' Oxford and 'The County Town' Aylesbury. It was a kind of milestone code.

Some milestones were placed high up on a wall, which was convenient for the main users of the roads, carters, coachmen and people on horseback, but awkward for

anyone on foot. So, too, were the obelisk milestones. One of the tallest of these, nearly fifteen metres high, stands outside the Imperial War Museum, in south-east London. Nowadays, distances to London are measured to the statue of Charles I in Trafalgar Square.

Eighteenth- and nineteenth-century milestones were of many types. The ones put up by the famous road engineer, Thomas Telford, in the early nineteenth century were flat and pointed and looked very much like tombstones. Many of the Victorian ones were more elaborate. A favourite design, which continued until well into the present century, was triangular, with a sloping top, made in cast iron. A large number of these are still to be seen.

Signposts

Until the late eighteenth century, Britain's roads were not well signposted. A few earlier signposts have survived. There is one supposed to date back to 1669 at the top of Broadway Hill in Worcestershire.

Most of the signposts we see today are fairly modern, unless they happened to be made of iron or stone. Wooden signposts rot and have to be replaced every fifty years or so, sometimes more often.

There has been very little change in the design of

signposts during the past two hundred years, except that many of them, especially on the main roads, are much lower than they used to be in the days of horses. The most convenient height for a signpost that can be read by a car driver is just over a metre from the ground and that is what it usually is now, although lorry and coach drivers would probably prefer something a little higher.

Some signposts direct people to places of interest in towns and villages. A sign in Bath points to 'Hot Springs and Roman Baths', and all over Britain there are signs telling people the way to public lavatories, post offices, railway stations, bus stations and other important places. Modern, fast-moving motor traffic has to have a different kind of signpost, with large clear letters, at right angles to the flow of traffic. This is the motorway type.

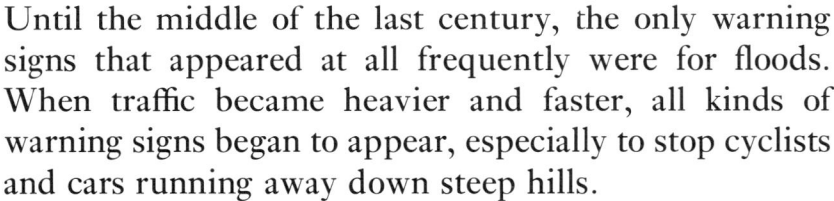

Warning signs

Until the middle of the last century, the only warning signs that appeared at all frequently were for floods. When traffic became heavier and faster, all kinds of warning signs began to appear, especially to stop cyclists and cars running away down steep hills.

At first, only words were used, but symbols were added after the 1914–18 war. Warning signs were standardised early on the Continent, but until 1964 all kinds of strange signs were used in Britain.

The development of motorways from the 1950s onwards produced a great increase in the number and range of illuminated signs, warning drivers of fog, accidents, ice, roadworks and so on.

Riding and driving

Traffic lights

The first electrically operated traffic lights were set up in the United States in the early 1920s. They were invented by an American with the very suitable name of Flex. London had traffic lights in 1928 and by the 1930s, with the rapid increase in motor traffic, they were to be found in most large towns. Over the years, the pattern of the lights themselves has changed very little, but there have been great improvements in the control equipment and in the sensing pads in the road, over which vehicles have to pass. Many traffic lights are now computer-controlled, to give a more even flow of traffic. Television cameras have been installed at some of the busiest road junctions in London and other big cities, so that controllers can watch the build-up of traffic and use the lights to control the flow of traffic in the best possible way, minute by minute.

The electronic control boxes placed near the traffic lights normally work automatically. They can be re-set to meet changing conditions at different times of the day and, if necessary, put out of action altogether, so that police or wardens can sort out traffic jams in the old-fashioned way by means of hand signals.

Parking meters
and parking signs

Parking meters were introduced into Britain from America in the 1950s. Once they became common, it was necessary to have special traffic wardens to patrol the area, partly to make sure that motorists had not run out of their time at the meter and partly to discover and fine people who had parked in forbidden places, instead of at a meter.

If they are to be of any use, parking meters have to be solidly built and reliable. They are, in fact, among the strongest and best designed pieces of modern street furniture that we have.

Signs telling motorists where and when they are allowed and not allowed to park are, like one-way signs and speed restriction signs, a very important type of street furniture today. In recent years, there has been a movement to make these signs as bold and simple as possible, so that their message can be taken in at a glance by the driver of a moving vehicle.

An elaborate system of road-markings continues the task of telling the motorist where and when he is allowed to stop.

Bus stops and bus shelters

In Britain wherever there are buses, there are signs to tell people where they stop and, in many cases, at what times. Bus signs are an important part of the street scene and over the years there have been many experiments to make them easier to see and to distinguish the different kinds of stopping places – fare stages, request stops, setting-down-only stops and so on.

In towns, there were very few bus shelters in existence until about thirty years ago, but since then they have appeared everywhere, probably because most people no longer wear the kind of clothes that protect them against the wind, cold and rain. Rural bus shelters have been with us for a good deal longer. Before the Second World War, many of them were paid for by well-to-do local people, often in memory of a member of their family, or by the Women's Institute or Parish Council. Some were solidly built and very charmingly designed, to fit in with the surroundings.

Grit bins

In the days of horse traffic, grit was needed in the winter months to stop horses from slipping and falling on icy roads and to allow them to get a grip on hills. The sand or fine gravel was often just left in piles by the roadside but in cities bins were in use a hundred years ago. Most towns now have some grit bins, although the usual practice is to send a gritting lorry to make the roads safe and to keep the sand or grit in the bins for the pavements.

Walking

Beacons and pedestrian crossings

The familiar illuminated beacons at pedestrian crossings – orange glass globes with a flashing light inside – were introduced, like pedestrian crossings themselves, in the mid-1930s. They were called Belisha beacons, after Leslie Hore-Belisha, who was Minister of Transport at the time.

Pedestrian crossings – zebra crossings – have only the beacons to warn drivers to slow and stop. Pelican crossings have green, amber and red signals and are controlled by pedestrians themselves, by pressing a button to stop the traffic.

Bollards

Bollards, made of cast iron, wood or, later, concrete, have been used from the seventeenth century onwards to keep vehicles away from places where they were not supposed to go and to protect pedestrians from the traffic. Most iron bollards date from the nineteenth century. Many of the earlier ones were made from cannon muzzles, with the ends filled up with iron domes. Some nineteenth-century bollards have dates on them.

Bollards with rings on them were also used as hitching posts for horses. Others were placed against gateways or entrances to buildings, to stop the walls being damaged by carriages and carts taking the corner too fast.

The commonest kind of modern bollard is the illuminated type that we see on traffic islands.

Railings

Most of the eighteenth- and nineteenth-century railings
that are still to be seen are around the top of basement-
wells and along high paths, where it would be easy to fall
over the edge if the railings weren't there.

There are other purposes for railings nowadays. One
of these is to prevent people from crossing the street at
dangerous places, like road junctions. Another is to stop
children from rushing straight out of the playground and
into the road and the traffic when they come out of school.

A special type of railing is the very strong rail of
galvanised steel fixed down the central division of a
motorway to stop vehicles out of control from crossing
over into the other carriageway and crashing headlong
into vehicles travelling in the opposite direction. The
same sort of railing is often put along sharp bends,
especially on mountain roads, to prevent cars and lorries
from going over the edge of a steep drop and possibly into
a ravine.

Seats and benches

Most of the older seats in parks and streets date from the nineteenth century, when local councils and private individuals began to pay for seats and benches to be installed wherever people might be likely to be walking about and needing a rest. They usually had cast-iron frames, with wooden seats and backs bolted to them. The designers often produced strange and fanciful designs for the frames. A series on the Victoria Embankment in London has the frames cast in the form of crouching camels. Iron tree branches and plants were common patterns.

Litter bins

Fifty years ago there wasn't as much litter about as there is today, and the streets were swept more regularly. Now, however, when nearly everything we buy comes in a package of some kind, litter bins are very necessary and there are many more of them. Bins more than twenty or thirty years old are rare. The thin metal rusts away and the bins have to be replaced.

Street lighting

Lanterns and gas

The first street to be lit experimentally by gas was in Birmingham in 1802. Before that street lighting had been a very patchy and unsatisfactory affair. People who lived in the bigger and more expensive houses were often ordered to put lanterns and candles outside to help passers-by to see their way, but the lights, when they existed, often went out, especially in bad weather.

London got its first gas lighting in 1807, when thirteen elegant iron lamp-posts, each fitted with three globes, were put up in Pall Mall. These have now vanished, but bracket lamps of about the same period are still to be seen off Pall Mall, in Crown Court and Mall Passage. By 1823 there were more than 30,000 gas lights in London.

Many of the early gas lamps, most of them now converted to electricity, are still to be found in alleyways and courts. Different towns and cities developed their own special styles of lamp-posts. You can usually tell if a lamp standard is old or modern. The old ones, especially those put up in Victorian times, are mostly heavy, solid affairs, often with a good deal of ornamentation. Iron was cheap then and the Victorians used plenty of it. Modern street-lighting standards are plainer and more slender.

Electricity

Apart from earlier experiments, the first use of electric lighting in British streets – the Americans were a year or two earlier – was in 1879, when a mile and a quarter of London streets, from Westminster to Waterloo, was lit by forty electric lights. Many of the lamp standards are still there.

One of the earliest provincial towns to go in for electric street lighting was Taunton, in 1885. The two-globed lamp standards are still there and still in use.

Some of the most interesting lamps, both for gas and electricity, were designed to hang from brackets outside shops, hotels, public houses and restaurants. They were used to advertise the business, as well as to light the pavement and the entrance. Not many of these are left. Sometimes the brackets remain, but the lights have gone or been replaced by modern ones.

Perhaps the best known bracket lamps are the Blue Lamps fixed outside police stations. Some old examples of these are still on the original building, but others have been moved to new police stations, where they are easily recognised.

Quite a lot of today's street-lighting standards were originally put up to support the overhead electricity wires for trams and trolley-buses. The trams and the wires disappeared many years ago, but the thrifty local authorities left the iron or steel poles in position and fixed modern electric lighting units to the top, usually of the type which works by passing an electric current through sodium vapour. This is cheaper than the bulb-type of light, lasts longer and provides better illumination in fog. The higher above the ground the lamp is, the greater the distance it throws its light and the easier it is to avoid dark patches between one light and the next.

27

Water supply and sanitation
Public lavatories

London began to have a sewerage system in the 1850s and the first public lavatories came into existence then. In 1851, at the Great Exhibition at the Crystal Palace in Hyde Park, the pioneer in the manufacture of these appliances, George Jennings, was allowed to build conveniences where people were charged a penny a head – the phrase 'to spend a penny' dates from then.

By the 1870s public lavatories were being installed all over Britain. Many of them, for gentlemen only, were made of cast iron, elaborately decorated and often in the shape of Indian or Greek temples. Round urinals of this type are now very rare.

A little later, in the 1880s, more solid structures of brick or stone were being built, with accommodation for both ladies and gentlemen. Some of these looked like little Tudor cottages or medieval castles.

The first underground lavatory was provided, also by Jennings, at the Royal Exchange in London in the 1860s. By the 1890s, there were a great many of them, palaces of marble, brass and glass.

Many underground lavatories are now in a dilapidated state, and a number have had to be closed because of the destruction caused by vandals.

Fire hydrants

Before towns had a piped water supply, the only way of trying to put out a fire was with buckets. Even if the fire happened to be conveniently near a river or a pond, the old-fashioned hoses, made of leather or canvas, didn't allow you to pump water from very far away, especially in the days when all the pumping had to be done by hand. Fire hydrants, connected to the water mains, began to be set up in cities in the 1840s, and thirty years later there were hundreds of them. Sometimes the hydrant took the form of a standpipe fixed against the wall of a building or on the edge of the pavement, but more often the system was to have a socket under an iron lid in the pavement or roadway. In the case of a fire, all the fire brigade had to do was to take up the lid, fix a hose on to the socket and turn on the water. This is usually how it's done nowadays, although in most cities you can see solid-looking cast-iron standpipes near the kerb, ready to join a hose to in an emergency. If you notice a metal plate with an H on it fixed to the wall of a building near pavement level, that means there is a hydrant point close at hand under a cover. A number, say 8, under the letter H means the hydrant is eight feet away from the plate.

Manhole covers and gratings

The most attractive type of road-level furniture is the coal-hole cover. These cast-iron covers had to have a rough surface, so that pedestrians should not slip on them when the pavement was wet or icy. This encouraged the manufacturers to ornament them with elaborate designs, which often included the maker's name and address.

As well as coal-hole covers, there is a great variety of inspection covers for all types of services – telephone circuits, gas and water mains, electric cables, hydrants and sewers. Heavy lorries have caused a great deal of damage to these covers, especially those over sewers, and a stronger type is now being installed.

Underground street drains were introduced about a hundred and fifty years ago, but only in the major roads

of important towns. Once the drains were there, there
had to be some way of letting the surface water run into
them, without having dangerous holes in the road or
pavement. The answer was to fix strong cast-iron grids
over the hole, so that the water could flow down, but
people, animals and rubbish were kept out. During the
twentieth century, a different system began to be used,
with the hole down into the drain set by the side of the
gutter and under the kerb.

Metal gratings, let into the pavement, have been used
for three hundred years to allow light into basements and
at the same time to protect pedestrians from falling down
into the basement area.

Metal-framed pavement lights, with cut squares of heavy glass fitted into an iron grid, date from the 1880s. In recent years, the normal practice has been to use smaller lenses set in reinforced concrete. These withstand heavy traffic loads without damage.

Drinking-water furniture – humans and animals

Before piped water was laid on to nearly every building, if you wanted water for washing, cooking or drinking, you had to go and fetch it from a well, a pump or a fountain. Few of these are now in use, but many can still be seen, often with a little building or shelter over them. They were favourite gossiping places, where women met their neighbours every day when they went to draw water.

Public drinking fountains are to be found everywhere. Most of them were erected in the nineteenth century and some are very grand. The old type of drinking fountain was not very hygienic. It usually had an iron drinking cup, fixed to a chain, and everybody used it.

These public drinking fountains were erected partly to provide people with pure water to drink, at a time when much of the drinking water available, especially from wells and pumps, was dangerous to health, partly as memorials to local residents, and partly by the Temperance Movement, to persuade people to drink water, instead of beer or spirits.

Until the early nineteenth century, cattle, horses and dogs had to make do with rivers, ponds or water in buckets. In the country this wasn't too difficult, but in towns water was often hard to find. So in the 1820s the Animal Protection Society, which later became the Royal Society for the Prevention of Cruelty to Animals, began setting up drinking troughs in London and by the 1860s the Metropolitan Drinking Fountain Association was doing the same. These troughs sometimes formed part of drinking fountains for humans.

Like the drinking fountains, a number of drinking troughs for animals were provided as memorials.

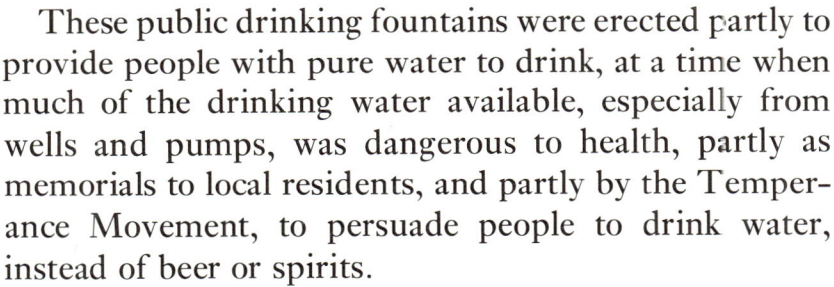

Communications

Posting boxes

Letters originally had to be handed in at post offices. The first pillar boxes in the British Isles were set up in 1852 in the Channel Islands. They were six-sided, over a metre high and made of cast iron. To give them extra height, they were mounted on blocks of granite. They had a vertical posting-slot – not horizontal, as it is nowadays – and the Royal Arms on three of the sides.

By 1853, pillar boxes were being installed all over Britain. They looked very much like the ones in Jersey and Guernsey, except they were taller and had no need of a stone block to bring the slot up to a convenient level for posting. Their successors, put up during the late 1850s and the 1860s, were of several different types, some fluted, like stone columns, some six-sided, some very plain and simple, some very decorated. Two of these early pillar boxes are shown here, one on this page, and one on the bottom right of page 37. The pillar boxes designed from 1879 onwards were mostly round or oval. From 1899 onwards, boxes with two posting-slots were often found. One slot was usually for local mail, the other for letters going to other parts of Britain.

Pillar boxes have changed less than any other kind of street furniture. Those designed during the reign of Elizabeth II look very much the same as the ones set up in the time of her great-great-grandmother, Queen

Victoria. Only the royal cipher has changed with each new king or queen. There have been three of these royal ciphers altogether: VR (Victoria Regina, Queen Victoria); ER (Eduardus Rex, Edward VII, and Elizabeth Regina, Elizabeth II); and GR (Georgius Rex, George V and George VI). Edward VIII, who ruled for little more than a year, had no pillar boxes bearing his cipher.

Cast-iron boxes fixed in walls and bolted to wooden posts or lamp-posts were first used in 1858. They were smaller and cheaper than free-standing pillar boxes. Many of them are still to be found in towns and cities, but most of them are in country districts.

Stamp-vending machines

Machines which sold stamps were put up unofficially between 1884 and 1887. In 1889 the Postmaster-General gave his approval for Collins' Automatic Stamp Deliverer to be set up by the side of some pillar boxes in London and by the 1890s these machines were to be found all over the country. They were supplied and maintained by the Stamp Distribution Syndicate, not by the Post Office, and they provided penny stamps on one side and halfpenny stamps on the other. Since then, new types of machine have been introduced to sell books of stamps.

Public telephones

Very few private individuals and by no means all businesses had telephones before the mid-1920s. The postal service was quick and reliable and telegrams were cheap. Some shops and hotels were prepared to allow people to make telephone calls from their premises and were often supplied by the Post Office with a blue and white sign, to be fixed outside, saying 'Public Telephone'. Many of these signs are still to be seen, although there is no longer a public telephone inside the building. A new yellow and black sign, saying 'Pay Phone' indicates a place where there is a coin-box phone today.

Telephone boxes, installed by the Post Office, first came into use in 1922, but there were not many of them

about until the 1930s. The original ones were made of wood, painted brown, with glass panels. Some of these, nearly fifty years old, are still in use today at railway stations and post offices, although in most cases the doors have been removed. Since then there have been a number of different types. Most of them were made with cast-iron side frames and roof, but some used concrete. The more recent type has one large pane of glass in each side, instead of a number of small panes. Most telephone boxes are painted red, like pillar boxes, but green and yellow ones are seen quite often, where these colours are considered to fit in better with the surroundings. Until 1939, nearly all calls had to be obtained through an operator, who told the caller how much money to put in the box. Automatic call-boxes were found very little before the 1950s, even in large cities.

Telling the time

Sundials

There were public sundials long before there were public clocks. The earliest of them were cut in the stone of churches, but they were also found on the walls of inns and on pillars in market squares and other public places.

College Green, York, has a sundial on a pillar, with a stone seat round the base.

Many of these sundials on columns are so high up that they are difficult to read and must always have been more for ornament than for use. Sundials are still made, but mostly as garden ornaments. There is a modern public sundial at Greenwich, however.

Clocks

Very early clocks had no hands, the time being given only by a bell which chimed the hours and quarters. The next step forward was the single-handed clock. A splendid sixteenth-century one-handed clock, known as Matthew the Miller, on St Mary Steps Church in Exeter, has the hours struck by figures placed in niches.

Minute hands came into general use on public clocks during the eighteenth century. The hands were often made of wood, which rotted away or fell off in the course of years and had to be replaced. By 1800 practically every public building in the country had its clock. On town halls and large houses the clock was frequently on a little tower.

The clock on a house on the Guildford-Dorking road has a blacksmith hitting a bell with his hammer, with a message to travellers saying, 'By me you know how fast to go'. A clock with remarkable ironwork decorations was put up on the medieval walls of Chester in 1897 to celebrate Queen Victoria's Diamond Jubilee.

Clock at St Pancras Station, London

Clock on St Stephen's Church, Bristol

Jubilee Clock, Douglas, Isle of Man

Clock towers

The most famous clock tower in the world forms part of the Houses of Parliament in London and contains Big Ben. Many other clock towers have been modelled on it.

Many clock towers were constructed to mark Queen Victoria's Jubilees of 1887 and 1897. One of the finest is in North Street, Brighton. It has mosaic portraits of the Queen, Prince Albert, and the Prince and Princess of Wales, and underground public lavatories in its base. Another multi-purpose clock tower at Tynemouth has a drinking fountain and horse-trough at the bottom.

Clockgate Tower, Youghal, Co. Cork ▷

Bracket clocks

Clocks fixed to brackets which project from the front of buildings were first made in the mid-seventeenth century. They became very popular in Victorian times, despite the fact that it was awkward to set up a ladder to wind them, and a number of them received a new lease of life when it became possible to drive clocks by electricity and avoid the winding-up process.

Many bracket clocks serve as advertisements for shops or public houses. Watch and clockmakers' shops often had a clock outside made in the form of a huge gilded watch.

Digital clocks

In the past twenty years, a new kind of clock, the digital clock, has been developed, which has no dial or hands and shows the time as a row of figures. Most of the public clocks installed nowadays are of this type.

Railway and post office clocks

The railways and the postal services work very much by the clock, and their customers need to know the exact time in order to be sure of catching the train or the post. For this reason, even very small stations and post offices have always, until recently, considered it part of their duty to provide a public clock.

It is interesting to notice that public clocks of all types are much more common in Britain than in other countries. It is difficult to find a reason for this. Does time matter more here? Or do the British just like the look of a clock?

Statues and war memorials

There are very few towns without statues and memorials. Sometimes the statues are of nationally famous people, like explorers, scientists, great admirals and statesmen, sometimes of local worthies. There are plenty of kings and queens about, especially Queen Victoria. Most large towns have Queen Victoria in a prominent position.

Statues add to the interest of a town, although we may sometimes think our ancestors put them up to some pretty strange people.

War memorials, too, are an interesting part of local history, although in this case a very sad part. You can find them not only in towns, but in villages as well, with the men killed in three wars listed on them – the South African War, World War I and World War II. Quite often one memorial serves for two of these wars and sometimes for all three.

Index